A Summary of the Revelation of the Seven Seals

Jason DeMars

Presenting the teaching as revealed to God's servant, Brother William Branham.

2nd Edition

Copyright © 2017 Present Truth Ministries, Jason DeMars
All rights reserved.

ISBN: 9798878466530
Imprint: Independently published

Dedicated to all those righteous souls who are seeking to understand the Word of God with their whole heart.

CONTENTS

Introduction
- *Seven Seals Revealed* — 7

Chapter 1: Purpose of the Sealed Book
- *Seven Angels Meet the Prophet* — 9
- Timeline of Events — 10

Chapter 2: The First Seal
- *White Horse Rider* — 12

Chapter 3: The Second Seal
- *Red Horse Rider* — 15

Chapter 4: The Third Seal
- *Black Horse Rider* — 17

Chapter 5: The Fourth Seal
- *Pale Horse Rider* — 19

Chapter 6: The Fifth Seal
- *Souls Under the Altar* — 21

Chapter 7: The Sixth Seal
- *Interruption of Nature* — 23

Chapter 8: The Seventh Seal
- *Silence in Heaven* — 27
- Are the Seven Thunders Truly Revealed? — 29
- Rapturing Faith is in the Seven Thunders and Rapturing Faith is Being Laid Forth in the Messages — 32

- Seven Seals Are Revealed at the Time of the Seven Thunders	33
- Thunders Are Already in the Written Word	33
- Seven Thunders Are Revealed at the Time of the Opening of the Seals	35
- Examining the Scriptures of the Open Word	37
- Could It Be the Seventh Trumpet Angel?	42
- The Presence of the Son of Man	43
- The Bride Coming to the Fullness of Christ	45
- Eat the Book	48
- Conclusion	49

Addendum
- *Significance of the Opening of the Seven Sealed Book* 51

Bibliography 59

INTRODUCTION
Seven Seals Revealed

Daniel 12:4 *"But thou, O Daniel, shut up the words, and seal the book, even to the time of the end: many shall run to and fro, and knowledge shall be increased."*

Most Christians are unaware that in the Bible there is a promise of the revealing of the sealed book in the end time. Notice, that in Revelation 22:18-19 the canon of Scripture is closed. We may add no new revelation, neither may we take away from what is written. It is apparent that God is not seeking to bring new scripture or new revelation. However, the book of Revelation has been probed at and many have tried to understand it; many have injected their view and purported it as factual. It is clear from what the Lord spoke to Daniel that this revelation will not be revealed until the end time.

Just as God has done throughout the ages, he expanded the revelations given to his prophets, in a progressive way. In Revelation, chapter 5, we find that John was given a vision of heavenly things and witnessed a book, not only sealed but, sealed with seven seals. John received a prophetic vision of end time events. It is only the Lamb of God, our Lord Jesus Christ, that is worthy to take the book and loose the seals.

What then, is the purpose of loosing the seals? It is twofold: Thus, *firstly*, it is the book of redemption, which the Messiah purchased the right to at Calvary. *Secondly*, the book itself contains the revelation of the mysteries that were hidden in ages past; this book was connected to Messiah's death on the cross for our sins. I want to emphasize the words of the angel in Daniel 12:4, "… seal the book, even to the time of the end." Therefore, at the end time, just prior to the return of Christ, the revealing of the secrets of this book will be made known.

Notice, in Daniel 12 these things were communicated to a prophet by a mighty Angel. Revelation 10 shows us the same picture. The same Angel descended with an open book—the seals having been previously opened—and communicates it to a messenger of God: the seventh church age messenger, whom we know to be Brother William Branham. Revelation 10:3-4 shows that in the time of John there were mysteries hidden that were to be revealed at the end time. It is not to be anything outside of the Bible, rather the Bible clearly revealed. This mystery was to be revealed by Christ through the seventh church age messenger. With that said, let us go into the purpose of the sealed book.

CHAPTER 1

PURPOSE OF THE SEALED BOOK
Seven Angels Meet the Prophet

In December 1962 Brother William Branham had a vision about meeting seven angels in Arizona and a loud blast would accompany this; then he would be picked up into this constellation of angels. [i] February 28, 1963 [ii] a cloud formation appeared and was photographed. It was so high in the atmosphere that it baffled the experts. The photo represents seven angels on their way to meet Brother Branham. Approximately seven days later in March 1963 Bro. [iii] Branham heard a loud thunder and met the seven angels who commissioned him to return to his home city of Jeffersonville, Indiana, USA to preach "The Seven Seals." [iv] He returned and for a series of sermons these seven angels met with him, one by one, for each seal and he preached a sermon on each seal. Brother Branham said, "This SEVEN-SEALED BOOK is REVEALED at the TIME of the SEVEN THUNDERS of Revelations 10." [v]

He told us the book that was sealed is the Book of Redemption and this needed to be opened by the one who paid the price (the Lord Jesus Christ) to complete the process of redemption.

1 Peter 1:5 *"Who are kept by the power of God through faith unto salvation ready to be revealed in the last time."*

Since the time of the seals being broken, the mysteries of the Bible have now been revealed. Here is a summary of the seven seals, as they were revealed to Brother Branham.

This seven-sealed Book is revealed at the time of the Seven Thunders of Revelation 10.

Timeline of Events

1. December 22, 1962: WMB sees the vision of seven angels meeting him with a loud thunder near Tucson, Arizona

2. December 30, 1962: preaches "Is This the Sign of the End, Sirs?" to report the vision and speak of its basic meaning

3. February 28, 1963: mysterious cloud appears northeast of Tucson, Arizona

4. March 7 or 8, 1963: WMB hears loud thunder and is caught up into a constellation of seven angels

5. March 17 to 24, 1963: preaches "Revelation of the Seven Seals"

6. May 17, 1963: picture of the mysterious cloud is released in Life Magazine

CHAPTER 2

THE FIRST SEAL
White Horse Rider

Revelations 6:1-2 *"¹ And I saw when the Lamb opened one of the seals, and I heard, as it were the noise of thunder, one of the four beasts saying, Come and see. ² And I saw, and behold a white horse: and he that sat on him had a bow; and a crown was given unto him: and he went forth conquering, and to conquer."*

Before we go into the first seal, let's discuss verse one, because it sets the stage for the first four seals. When the Lamb opened the first seal there was a noise of thunder. So, corresponding to the opening of the first seal there is a thunder. The noise of the thunder is what was reported to have been heard when the Father was speaking to the Lord Jesus in John 12:29. The thunder speaks of the voice of God; and what can reveal the hidden mysteries contained in the seals besides the voice of God? It is important to note that when Brother Branham met the seven angels near Sunset Mountain outside of Tucson, Arizona in 1963, there was the noise of a thunder, as well. He heard it and so did the two brothers that were with him during that time.

Next, we see that one of the four beasts says, "Come and see." Why did one of the four beasts make this announcement to John?

Revelation 4:7 *"And the first beast was like a lion, and the second beast like a calf, and the third beast had a face as a man, and the fourth beast was like a flying eagle."*

This is the beast that was liken unto a lion. While the horse riders were bringing forth the deceptive work of Satan, these four beasts, as guardians of the throne, were the form with which the Holy Spirit worked in the church to combat the work of Satan. Brother Branham says regarding the lion, "Now, remember, now in the first age was a lion age...that roared, that pure unadulterated Word." This is the apostolic ministry, the second and third generation believers that stood firm with the apostolic doctrine.

"Notice, he was dressed in white which appears righteous; but he had a bow but no arrows meaning he was a bluff." Brother Branham taught us this was the spirit of Nicolaitianism that went forth in the first church as a doctrine. Nicolaitianism means to conquer the laity. They formed a hierarchy in the early church. Here is an example: Ignatius of Antioch, who was a bishop until the year 107 AD, writing to the Smyrnaens states, "See that ye all follow the bishop, even as Jesus Christ does the Father, and the presbytery as ye would the apostles; and reverence the deacons, as being the institution of God. Let no man do anything connected with the Church without the bishop." He goes on to say, "It is well to reverence both God and the bishop. He who honours the bishop has been honoured by God; he who does anything without the knowledge of the bishop, does [in reality] serve the devil. Nor is there anyone in the Church greater than the bishop, who ministers as a priest to God for the salvation of the whole world." This elevated the bishop of a church to a position higher than the believers and thus snuffed out the leadership of the Holy Spirit. The time- period of the first horse rider corresponds with the Ephesian Church Age.

*As a note: the seals do not correspond precisely to the Seven Church Ages. As you will recognize, the seals overlap; there is a blending into multiple ages.

CHAPTER 3

THE SECOND SEAL
Red Horse Rider

Revelation 6:3-4 *"³ And when he had opened the second seal, I heard the second beast say, 'Come and see.' ⁴ And there went out another horse that was red: and power was given to him that sat thereon to take peace from the earth, and that they should kill one another: and there was given unto him a great sword."*

The second beast was like a calf or an ox. This is the form that the Spirit of God took in this age to combat the red horse rider. Brother Branham said:

"Now, the second beast that the antichrist sent out was a red beast, which was a—that he rode on—was to take peace from the earth and—and war. Now, the second one that went to combat him was the ox beast. The ox means a labor, a beast of burden."

The Spirit came upon the people in such a way that they were willing to lay down their lives as martyrs. This was the strength given to them to overcome during the riding of the red horse.

Notice power was given to him: that doctrine of Nicolaitianism became incarnate in a man that was elected to be over the people. That took place when men elected a papacy to rule the hearts of men instead of the Holy Ghost to rule the hearts of men. Recognize, the horse was red, signifying the killing of those who opposed. The first church of Rome became apostate early on, after the Jews were expelled from Rome, in the mid-1st century. It later began cooperating with Imperial Rome and took part in persecuting the true church until it was almost completely stamped out in Western Europe. This corresponds to the Smyrnaen and Pergamaen Church Ages where the true church was persecuted by the false Roman Church, working together with Imperial Rome.

CHAPTER 4

THE THIRD SEAL
Black Horse Rider

Revelation 6:5-6 *"⁵ And when he had opened the third seal, I heard the third beast say, 'Come and see.' And I beheld, and lo a black horse; and he that sat on him had a pair of balances in his hand. ⁶ And I heard a voice in the midst of the four beasts say, 'A measure of wheat for a penny, and three measures of barley for a penny; and see thou hurt not the oil and the wine.'"*

The third beast had the face of a man. Brother Branham told us, "The next come, was a man, was a Beast with a face of a man. And that man was the reformers, man's education, theology, and so forth." It was the wisdom of the reformers that overcame what the black horse rider did.

Brother Branham said this black horse represents famine for the Word, because black represents famine; and the scales in his hand, he said, represented it had turned to money. "This black horse was riding, when they charged for their sacrifices and everything they done, and money was just... oh, you know how it was. And that is the history of the Catholic church." This corresponds to what is referred to as the Dark Ages or

Middle Ages, wherein the Roman Catholic Church ruled the leaders of western Europe and controlled religion and politics and, as such, economics. It is the same time-period as the Thyatiran Church Age leading into the Sardisian Church Age wherein The Reformation began.

CHAPTER 5

THE FOURTH SEAL
Pale Horse Rider

Reelation 6:7-8 *"⁷ And when he had opened the fourth seal, I heard the voice of the fourth beast say, 'Come and see.' ⁸ And I looked, and behold a pale horse: and his name that sat on him was Death, and Hell followed with him. And power was given unto them over the fourth part of the earth, to kill with sword, and with hunger, and with death, and with the beasts of the earth."*

Brother Branham taught us the brindle color was all the colors we've seen (white, red and black) in this horse mixed together, "… antichrist spirit, formed an organization, gave birth to some daughters of organization, changing his power three times, and put them in one, and made a pale horse, and then given a name called Death, and rode him into eternity. Just as plain as it can be." The time-period of the riding of this horse is the Laodicean Church Age when the ecumenical movement started with the deceptions of the Roman Catholic Church to bring all the Protestants back under her power. This is the church spoken of in Revelation 3:20, that put Christ on the outside.

The fourth beast that was sent to combat this working of Satan is the eagle.

"But now when it comes forth, the eagle age; that's the one that God always likens His prophets to eagles. He calls Himself an eagle. The eagle goes so high there ain't nothing else can touch him. Not only is he up there, but he's built for that position. When he gets up there, he see where he's at."

The Spirit that empowers the church to overcome is in the form of the eagle, which allows us to raise up high above the things of the world, to see the revelation and to soar in the heavenlies.

The first four seals deal with the church and how that spirit of Nicolaitianism came in first as a doctrine, then incarnated in a man—the Pope—began destroying the leadership of the Holy Spirit for the people, and then ate away at the very foundation of the church until almost nothing was left. Therefore, the first four seals deal with the condition of the church and how it got that way. The 5th Seal deals with the Jews and the 6th Seal deals with God's wrath.

CHAPTER 6

THE FIFTH SEAL
Souls Horse Rider

Revelation 6:9-11 *"⁹ And when he had opened the fifth seal, I saw under the altar the souls of them that were slain for the word of God, and for the testimony which they held: ¹⁰ And they cried with a loud voice, saying, 'How long, O Lord, holy and true, dost thou not judge and avenge our blood on them that dwell on the earth?' ¹¹ And white robes were given unto every one of them; and it was said unto them, that they should rest yet for a little season, until their fellowservants also and their brethren, that should be killed as they were, should be fulfilled."*

Now, Brother Branham told us this speaks of the Jews that were martyred under the various persecutions upon the Jews, throughout the church ages. Notice, they sought vengeance, and they were called servants, not bride. These were not martyrs for Christ but were martyrs for the testimony which they held. These were Orthodox Jews that stood faithful to the Law of Moses, never having heard the gospel, and having been blinded to it as God turned to deal almost exclusively with the Gentiles. They were martyred for their race and faith and were given white robes. The second part deals with the persecution upon the Jews that will take place in the Great Tribulation.

Romans 11:1-2 *"¹ I say then, Hath God cast away his people? God forbid. For I also am an Israelite, of the seed of Abraham, of the tribe of Benjamin. ² God hath not cast away his people which he foreknew. Wot ye not what the scripture saith of Elias? how he maketh intercession to God against Israel, saying,"*

God has not cast away his people that he foreknew. He never casts his elect away. He will always use all means necessary to save his elect. Romans 11:32 says that he "... con-cluded them all in unbelief." But remember, Paul was a Jew, Peter was a Jew, etc. So, the Jews, that believed, were clearly not cast off; they were saved. The Jews under the fifth seal are elected Jews, chosen of God before the foundation of the world to be saved. They were faithful Orthodox Jews their entire lives, and did not have the testimony of Jesus Christ.

CHAPTER 7

THE SIXTH SEAL
Interruption of Nature

Revelation 6:12-17 *"*^{12}* And I beheld when he had opened the Sixth seal, and, lo, there was a great earthquake; and the sun became black as sackcloth of hair, and the moon became as blood;* ^{13} *And the stars of heaven fell unto the earth, even as a fig tree casteth her untimely figs, when she is shaken of a mighty wind.* ^{14} *And the heaven departed as a scroll when it is rolled together; and every mountain and island were moved out of their places.* ^{15} *And the kings of the earth, and the great men, and the rich men, and the chief captains, and the mighty men, and every bondman, and every free man, hid themselves in the dens and in the rocks of the mountains;* ^{16} *And said to the mountains and rocks, 'Fall on us, and hide us from the face of him that sitteth on the throne, and from the wrath of the Lamb:* ^{17} *For the great day of his wrath is come; and who shall be able to stand?'"*

In the sixth seal we witness several events: 1. an earthquake 2. an eclipse of the sun 3. a blood moon 4. meteors. As a result, it appears to mankind that the sky is being rolled up so-as to change its very nature, the earthquake being so great that mountains crumble from the volcanic eruptions and islands disappear from the shifting plates of earth's crust. Such a fear comes upon the earth that they hide themselves from Christ. Instead of repenting and turning to him with their whole heart, they run and hide from his call to repentance.

Brother Branham tells us that the sixth seal does not concern the Bride of Christ: she has been raptured. It concerns the Jews and those who are alive during the tribulation period. In fact, it's the tribulation period leading into the day of the Lord where there is an interruption of nature and great wrath poured out. Let's read another instance of darkness coming upon the world.

Exodus 10:21-23 *"²¹ And the LORD said unto Moses, Stretch out thine hand toward heaven, that there may be darkness over the land of Egypt, even darkness which may be felt. ²² And Moses stretched forth his hand toward heaven; and there was a thick darkness in all the land of Egypt three days: ²³ They saw not one another, neither rose any from his place for three days: but all the children of Israel had light in their dwellings."*

God, through his prophet, Moses, called darkness upon the land of Egypt. It was God, indeed, that brought the darkness; but he used his prophet to indicate the precise purpose the darkness comes. In the tribulation period, God will use the two witnesses of Revelation 11 to be the means to reveal the precise reason that it comes. Note the following Scriptures:

Revelation 11:3-6 *"³ And I will give power unto my two witnesses, and they shall prophesy a thousand two hundred and threescore days, clothed in sackcloth. ⁴*

These are the two olive trees, and the two candlesticks standing before the God of the earth. ⁵ And if any man will hurt them, fire proceedeth out of their mouth, and devoureth their enemies: and if any man will hurt them, he must in this manner be killed. ⁶ These have power to shut heaven, that it rain not in the days of their prophecy: and have power over waters to turn them to blood, and to smite the earth with all plagues, as often as they will."

The prophecies bring forth the interruption of nature. Remember, it was Elijah that prophesied that no rain would come forth; and it was Moses that turned the water into blood and smote the earth with plagues. It will not literally be these men, but contemporary Jewish men that are sent in the spirit of power: one of Elijah and the other of Moses. What a great and mighty shaking that will take place. Notice, just after the resurrection of these two witnesses and their being caught up to heaven, the same terminology is used: a great earthquake takes place.

Revelation 11:13 *"And the same hour was there a great earthquake, and the tenth part of the city fell, and in the earthquake were slain of men seven thousand: and the remnant were affrighted, and gave glory to the God of heaven."*

Remarks by Brother Branham, concluding his thoughts upon the sixth seal:

"What is it? What can bring these things but the Word? They can do nature any way they want to. Here it is. They're the one who brings on this Sixth Seal. They *uncover and open it up. It's the power of God to interrupt nature. See, the Sixth Seal, is completely an interruption of nature. Do you get it now? There's your Seal. Who does it? It's the prophets the other side of the rapture. With the power of God, the Word of God, they just condemn nature. They can send earthquakes, turn the moon into blood, the sun can go down or anything at their command. Amen."* [vi]

CHAPTER 8

THE SEVENTH SEAL
Silence in Heaven

Revelation 8:1 *"And when he had opened the seventh seal, there was silence in heaven about the space of half an hour."*

Bro. Branham tells us that the seventh seal is in reference to the coming of the Lord for his church. He equates this seventh seal to Revelation 10 and Mark 13:32. He says it is the coming of the Lord because no man knows the day or the hour in which Christ will return, not even Christ himself (Mark 13:32). When the seal was opened there was a reverent hush in heaven. The silence illustrates that even the angels are in great anticipation for what is to take place, just as they are for the coming of the Lord. This silence and anticipation also corresponds to Revelation 10:1-7 where the seven thunders utter their voices. The coming of the Lord is not known and neither were the seven thunders known. So, it's connected. As Brother Branham stated:

"Even the Angels didn't understand it. See, He didn't reveal it. That's the reason, under our seventh mystery, when the seventh seal was opened, there was silence. Jesus, when He was on earth, they wanted to know

when He would come. He said, 'It's not... even the Son Himself don't know when it's going to happen.' See, God has this all to Himself. It's a secret. And that's the reason there was silence in Heaven for a space of half hour, and seven thunders utter their voices, and John was even forbidden to write it, see, the Coming of the Lord." [vii]

Therefore, it is the message of the seven thunders, that actually breaks this reverent silence revealing the hidden mystery.

Firstly, the Mighty Angel (which is Christ, in Spirit form) comes down with an open book and lets out a shout; secondlyt, seven thunders utter their voices—which are the seven angels that met bro. Branham in Arizona and then in Jeffersonville as each seal was revealed—and lastly, the seventh church age messenger finished the mystery of God which was hidden for ages. Christ came down in Spirit form to reveal himself to his Bride prior to the rapture. 1 Thessalonians 4:16 tells us the Lord comes down from heaven with a shout, the voice of the archangel and with the trump of God. Brother Branham states, "A shout, what is the shout? It's the Message going forth, first, the living Bread of Life bringing forth the Bride." [viii] Malachi 4:5-6, which we have covered in other articles, speaks of the two-fold coming of Elijah: once, before the first coming of Christ; and another time, before his second coming. The spirit of Elijah that was in Brother Branham was a ministry that "turns the hearts of the children to their fathers." According to Matthew 17:11, Elijah will restore all things. John the Baptist came and turned the hearts of the fathers to the children, but dispensationally he did not restore anything. In fact, he brought the believers of his day into a transition from the Old Covenant unto the New Covenant. Jesus said, "The law and the prophets were until John: since that time the kingdom of God is preached." [ix] The kingdom of heaven that was preached, was the one that was within them, which is the new covenant that John the Baptist and Jesus were in the process of introducing and which Jesus would finally make in his own blood. Then, at the day of Pentecost, the Spirit of God came and began writing the word of God on the hearts of the people. That was not a restoration message, it was a new message. At the end time, after the church falls away from the full apostolic doctrines, God sent a prophet in the spirit of Elijah to restore us back to the original faith.

"Now this messenger of Malachi 4 and Revelation 10:7 is going to do TWO things. One: According to Malachi 4 he will turn the hearts of the children to the fathers. Two: He will reveal the mysteries of the seven thunders in Revelation 10 which are the revelations contained in the seven seals. It will be these divinely revealed `mystery-truths that literally turn the hearts of the children to the Pentecostal fathers. Exactly so." [x]

Are the Seven Thunders Truly Revealed?

This is a question asked quite frequently and there are certain people that believe that the seven thunders are not revealed yet. Some say they are for the Jews and others say they are seven men that will thunder forth the mystery sometime in the future, just prior to the rapture. However, according to Brother Branham's clear and vindicated teaching, we believe that the seven thunders' voices have already been revealed. So, let's go through a few quotes and demonstrate the facts of this matter.

Before we do, I want to give my own personal testimony. I came to the Message in 1999 and first learned of the various teachings after reading An Exposition of the Seven Church Ages, I concluded that the seven thunders were revealed in the ministry of Brother Branham. I began to communicate this to a few people and they informed me I was in error and that they were not revealed yet. As a new believer I became confused. I began to study various understandings about Revelation chapter 10. One said, that only six seals are open and we are waiting for the seventh to be opened. Another said, everything is revealed except the seven thunders and we are just waiting on that. Each of these viewpoints could point us to quotes, but none of them could point you to, and give an explanation for, each of the statements by Brother Branham. All had varying reasons to avoid one quote or to throw out another quote. I was under this confusion for a long time until I decided, "I quit, I cannot figure it out and I need God to come and make it clear for me."

I was on a missionary trip to Turkey in the summer of 2013, still feeling unclear about the issue. My mind and heart were burdened, being desirous to give an explanation to the brothers and teach them the truth of this matter. I was riding down the street in a taxi, considering this issue, when I suddenly heard something speaking within me, "What order do these events take place in Revelation 10?" My response was, The Mighty Angel descends with an open book, then the seven thunders utter their voices and then the seventh angel finishes the mystery of God. Something within me spoke back, "Yes, that's right." Suddenly and instantly, the whole picture became clear. I already knew the Mighty Angel had descended and brought the opening of the word; and I already knew that the seventh angel sounded his voice to finish the mystery of God. So, if the seven thunders were in between the two, it had to be communicated to us through the seventh angel's message.

I went to the Scriptures and began to break this down. The Mighty Angel descends with this open book and cries out--from Greek it means preaching in a loud voice—as when a lion roars. What was he speaking about? Of course, he was communicating about the open book in his hand. But what were the results when he preached with a loud voice? The Scripture says, "… seven thunders uttered their voices." After Brother Branham preached the Seven Seals he made this statement, "Something happened the other day. You read the—or heard the tape, the seven thunders, "What Time Is It, Sir?" See? It happened the other day." What happened the other day? Seven angels met the prophet in the desert of Arizona and they came with a loud thunder, picking him up in the air, and commissioned him to preach on the Seven Seals. Then the mystery of God is finished because those seals are opened. What the seven thunders spoke was forbidden to be written down and were to be sealed up. If that mystery is to be finished and it was done so through the seventh angel then it is quite clear the thunders' voices have already been revealed. Now, let's go on through some quotes to tie it all together.

Rapturing Faith is in the seven thunders and rapturing faith is being laid forth in the messages

"And then there's coming forth seven mysterious thunders that's not even written at all. That's right. And I believe that through those seven thunders will be revealed in the last days in order to get the Bride together for rapturing faith; because what we got right now, we--we wouldn't be able to do it. There's something we've got to step farther; we--we can't have enough faith for Divine healing hardly. We've got to have enough faith to be changed in a moment and be swept up out of this earth, and we'll find that after a while, the Lord willing, find where it's written." [xi]

"And I remember when He swept down there in that big Light, standing yonder at the bottom of the river, 1933, in June, when He said, "As—as John the Baptist was sent forth and forerun the first coming of Christ; I send you with a Message to the world, to forerun the second Coming of Christ." And around the world She's went,

when revival fires had been built for fifteen years on nearly every mountain. Divine healing across the nations, and the power, and restoration.

226. And now I believe She is ready to strike that final climax yonder, to bring forth a Faith that will Rapture the Church into Glory. And She is laying in the Messages. We're really at the end time. We've talked about it, and everything, but the thing has moved upon us now. Yeah. Yes, sir. Here is one. That's right." [xii]

The second quote in this section was taken from a sermon preached prior to the opening of the Seven Seals. We understand that Brother Branham is telling us that rapturing faith is being built up. The messages in 1962 were laying the foundation for the seals to come. The final climax was going to come soon, "The Revelation of the Seven Seals."

Seven Seals are Revealed at the Time of the Seven Thunders

"This seven-sealed book is revealed at the time of the seven thunders of Revelations 10." [xiii]

Thunders are already in the Written Word

"And he said that this--in that day that he see Him come down, and he eat up the little book. And there

was... He put one foot on land and one on the sea and swore by Him that lives and ever and ever, that time shall be no more. And when He did, seven thunders uttered their voices. And when the seven thunders uttered their voices, John said he was about to write; and He said, "Don't write it." See? And he sealed it... what it is, is a "revelation" on what has been missed back there, to bring to... It's already wrote here; it's in here; it's to reveal what's already's been written (See?), 'cause you can't add one thing to It or take one word from It." [xiv]

"And then there's coming forth seven mysterious thunders that's not even written at all. That's right. And I believe that through those seven thunders will be revealed in the last days in order to get the Bride together for rapturing faith; because what we got right now, we--we wouldn't be able to do it. There's something we've got to step farther; we--we can't have enough faith for Divine healing hardly.

We've got to have enough faith to be changed in a moment and be swept up out of this earth, and we'll find that after a while, the Lord willing, find where it's written." [xv]

"Now, someone has been, many has been saying to me, and theologians said, 'Brother Branham, if the Lord God ...' Said, 'If--if with your experience that the Lord has given you for His people,' humbly saying this, said, 'you'd be eligible to write a--a Bible yourself, your Word that God has manifested.'

I said, That might be true. See, he was trying to catch me. See?

And I said, But, you see, I couldn't do that.

He said, 'Why couldn't you? You have all the qualifications.'

I said, But, you look, one word cannot be added or taken away. See?

And he said, 'Well then, them seven thunders (You see?),'

Said, 'wouldn't them seven thunders blasting out, won't that be a revelation be give to some man?'

I said, No, sir, it would be adding something to It or taking something from It. It's all revealed in there, and the seven seals opened up the revelation of what that was. See?" [xvi]

Seven Thunders Are Revealed At The Time of the Opening of the Seals

Q-395. *"Have the seven thunders which equals seven mysteries already been revealed? Were they revealed in the Seven Seals, but are yet-- but are yet not known to us as the thunders yet?"*

Answer: *"No, they were revealed in the seven seals; that's what the thunders was about. They was to reveal... The seven thunders that had uttered their voices and no one could make out what it was... John knew what it was, but he was forbidden to write it. He said, 'But the seventh angel in the days of his sounding, the seven mysteries of the seven thunders would be revealed.' And the seventh angel is a 'messenger' of the seventh church age. See?"* [xvii]

We begin to see the truth of the matter after studying these quotes closely. Here are the main points that we gather from the quotes to put the entire picture together:

1. Seven thunders will be revealed in the last days to get the Bride together for rapturing faith.

2. Rapturing faith lies in the messages that God delivers through his prophet.

3. Seven seals are revealed at the time of the Seven Thunders.

4. The thunders are not a new revelation, but are to reveal what is already written, hidden through the ages.

5. The seven seals illuminated the revelation of what the seven thunders are.

6. The thunders were revealed in the seven seals. The seventh messenger reveals what the seven mysteries of the seven thunders are.

We can conclude that the voices of the seven thunders are made know through the seventh angel's message. They've already been revealed under the revelation of the seven seals through the ministry of Brother William Branham: they are the contents of the open book which was sealed.

Examining the Scriptures of the Open Word

Let us now read the Scriptures we have so frequently referenced. These are the verses that are related to the seventh seal:

Revelation 10:1-7 *"¹ And I saw another mighty angel come down from heaven, clothed with a cloud: and a rainbow was upon his head, and his face was as it were the sun, and his feet as pillars of fire: ² And he had in his hand a little book open: and he set his right foot upon the sea, and his left foot on the earth, ³ And cried with a loud voice, as when a lion roareth: and when he had cried, seven thunders uttered their voices. ⁴ And when the seven thunders had uttered their voices, I was about to write: and I heard a voice from heaven saying unto me, Seal up those things which the seven thunders uttered, and write them not. ⁵ And the angel which I saw stand upon the sea and upon the earth lifted up his hand to heaven, ⁶ And sware by him that liveth for ever and ever, who created heaven, and the things that therein are, and the earth, and the things that therein are, and the sea, and the things which are therein, that there should be time no longer: ⁷ But in the days of the voice of the seventh angel, when he shall begin to sound, the mystery of God should be finished, as he hath declared to his servants the prophets."*

Here are several items noted in Revelation 10:
1. *the Mighty Angel*
2. *the open book*

3. *the Seven Thunders*
4. *the seventh angel*

Firstly, what is the Identity of the Mighty Angel? Let's examine who this Mighty Angel might be. He is clothed with a cloud. When God was leading the children of Israel out of Egypt God appeared in the form of a cloud by day. Secondly, a rainbow was upon his head. This is the covenant which God made with Noah. Not only that, but examine Revelation 4:2-3 where John sees the Almighty sitting upon his throne, "… there was a rainbow round about the throne." Thirdly, "his face was as it were the sun …" signifying that it was radiating with the shekinah glory of God. Fourthly, "his feet as pillars of fire …" which God appeared in the form of, when leading the children of Israel out of Egypt by night. This clearly identifies the Mighty Angel as the very theophany of God himself; it is none other than our Lord Jesus Christ. He descended in spirit form and had in his hand a little book open. This great Angel came down from heaven with the very book that Jesus Christ loosed the seals of. Next, he cries with a loud voice and when that happens it causes the seven thunders to utter their voices. Then John is told not to write what was said, that it would be sealed. To fully grasp what is taking place, we should go back to Daniel 12 to see the foundation of this vision.

Daniel 12:4 *"But thou, O Daniel, shut up the words, and seal the book, even to the time of the end: many shall run to and fro, and knowledge shall be increased."*

Daniel chapter 12 is where we find the first

discussion of a sealed book. The context is that Daniel has received various revelations that are in symbolic fashion and he is unsure of their meaning. He makes the request to receive an explanation for them:

Daniel 12:8 *"And I heard, but I understood not: then said I, 'O my Lord, what shall be the end of these things?'"*

This is the response he receives.

Daniel 12:9 *"And he said, 'Go thy way, Daniel: for the words are closed up and sealed till the time of the end.'"*

He was informed that he would not receive an answer, but an understanding would be given at the end time. An understanding of what? If you read the preceding chapters of Daniel you can realize it in regard to world empires, redemption and the final deliverance for the kingdom of Messiah to be set up. This is indeed "the mystery of God" denoting the redemption of man. Within this mystery are many mysteries, but they all come back to the one mystery of the sealed book. The first place we learn of the sealed book is in Daniel 12, but the sealed book appears again in Revelation 5.

Revelation 5:1-2 *"¹ And I saw in the right hand of him that sat on the throne a book written within and on the backside, sealed with seven seals. ² And I saw a strong angel proclaiming with a loud voice, Who is worthy to open the book, and to loose the seals thereof?"*

Now we find the book is not merely sealed, but it is sealed with seven seal. Only the Lamb is worthy to open the book. The Lamb's work pertains to redemption and this book is tied to redemption, based on Daniel 9-12. This is the Book of Redemption which is sealed up. What does being sealed up mean? It was hidden from Daniel's understanding, "I heard, but understood not."

Now, if this revelation came to a prophet, but was hidden, will this revelation come to the elect again? It must come through a prophet, once again. God has never, in one instance, revealed his word through a council of men or through a theological seminary.

When is the sealed book to be opened? Daniel 12:9 says, "the time of the end." Notice the next verse in Daniel:

Daniel 12:10 *"Many shall be purified, and made white, and tried; but the wicked shall do wickedly: and none of the wicked shall understand; but the wise shall understand."*

It says the WISE will understand. What will they understand? They will understand the hidden mysteries when the sealed book is opened. Let's think a little more about this. For this to go around the world and to reach the hearts of the people so that they can understand, there must be a period of time during which this revelation is made known. It cannot be done in mere hours, days or weeks. It must be an extended time-period so that the wise can understand, be purified and made white.

Let's start connecting Daniel 12 and Revelation 10 even further. In Revelation 10 we see a mighty angel clothed with a cloud, etc.; but in Daniel 12 we have another description:

Daniel 12:7 *"And I heard the man clothed in linen, which was upon the waters of the river, when he held up his right hand and his left hand unto heaven, and sware by him that liveth for ever that it shall be for a time, times, and an half; and when he shall have accomplished to scatter the power of the holy people, all these things shall be finished."*

This is just a partial description of the man clothed in linen that appeared previously in chapter 10 of Daniel. Below is a full description:

Daniel 10:5-6 *"⁵ Then I lifted up mine eyes, and looked, and behold a certain man clothed in linen, whose loins were girded with fine gold of Uphaz: ⁶ His body also was like the beryl, and his face as the appearance of lightning, and his eyes as lamps of fire, and his arms and his feet like in colour to polished brass, and the voice of his words like the voice of a multitude."*

Daniel describes the Man in his own words, as he saw him, in the vision and was inspired to do so; and John describes the Angel in his own words, with his own inspiration, and the description is similar.

In Daniel 12 the Man clothed in linen says it is sealed until the time of the end. Now, in Revelation 10 that same man—in the form of the Mighty Angel—comes down from heaven with an open book. The same one that sealed the book to Daniel, comes down with it open. He cries with a loud voice, obviously seeking to communicate what is in the open book. [As a reminder: 1 Thessalonians 4:16 says "... the Lord himself shall descend from heaven with a shout (the Message)] When he cries with the loud voice seven thunders utter their voices. Seven angels met bro. Branham and there was a loud thundering that took place. The seven thunders were sent to communicate what was in the open book. But when God reveals a certain thing it says he does so through his servants the prophets. It would take a messenger sent from God with a message to reveal what was in the open book. And the revelation of the mystery of God—the sealed book of redemption—comes to give us an understanding and purify us and make us white. Now, we are carrying this same Message around the world to find that last elect seed.

Could It Be the Seventh Trumpet Angel?

Regarding Revelation 10:7, it cannot be the trumpet angel because this messenger is clearly bringing a revelation. He is not merely blowing a trumpet to make a loud sound and bring forth the judgement of God, but he is communicating a revelation of the open book mystery. Revelation 11:15 is the seventh trumpet angel, which ushers in the day of the Lord and the millennial reign of

Christ. God is not repeating himself regarding the seventh trumpet angel. They have two distinct works, Revelation 10:7 says that through his voice the mystery is finished. And Revelation 11:15 is telling us that the kingdoms of this world has become the kingdoms of our Lord and of his Messiah. One is completing the revelation—giving an understanding—hidden from Daniel; and the other is the actual winding up of the great tribulation and ushering in of the millennial reign.

The Presence of the Son of Man

We have mentioned, in passing, that the seventh seal is connected to the coming of the Lord. The traditional viewpoint about the coming of the Lord is that it will be a sudden event. However, as we read in Scripture and study the truth of the matter, it becomes quite clear that it is connected to a series of events and takes place over time. To find the reality of this truth, let's study a few scriptures in the gospels.

Luke 17:22-30 "²² And he said unto the disciples, 'The days will come, when ye shall desire to see one of the days of the Son of man, and ye shall not see it. ²³ And they shall say to you, See here; or, see there: go not after them, nor follow them. ²⁴ For as the lightning, that lighteneth out of the one part under heaven, shineth unto the other part under heaven; so shall also the Son of man be in his day. ²⁵ But first must he suffer many things, and be rejected of this generation. ²⁶ And as it was in the days of Noe, so shall it be also in the days of the Son of man. ²⁷ They did eat, they drank, they married wives, they were given in marriage, until the day that Noe entered into the ark, and the flood came, and destroyed them all. ²⁸ Likewise also as it was in the days of Lot; they did eat, they drank, they bought, they sold, they planted, they builded; ²⁹ But the same day that Lot went out of Sodom it rained fire and brimstone from heaven, and destroyed them all. ³⁰ Even thus shall it be in the day when the Son of man is revealed.'"

The first thing I want to remind you of is the similarity of these verses regarding what is recorded in Matthew.

***Matthew 24:37** "But as the days of Noe were, so shall also the coming of the Son of man be."*

There is a parallel between these verses. Notice, Luke uses the "days of the Son of man" whereas Matthew uses "the coming of the Son of man." These are two different terms with two different meanings, but they are one and the same event looking at it from different angles. Note, that it says "days" of the Son of man. This signifies a time-period, not an instantaneous event. What happened in the days of Noah? Noah was sent with a message and preached to that generation so that they could be saved by getting into the ark. People went on living as though nothing was to occur. It will be the same at the end time: a man will be sent with a message so that people can be saved from the wrath to come and they continue living as though nothing will occur. The term used by Matthew is the Greek word "parousia". It means "presence". Thus, we can equate the "days of the Son of man" with the "presence of the Son of man." As we have already demonstrated, he descends from heaven with a message, an open book. So, today, he is here: he is present with his Bride. Luke 17:30 is an oft quoted passage of Brother Branham where he references the days of Lot with the time that the Lord met Abraham and revealed the secrets of the heart to Sarah. This same thing took place in our day through the ministry of Brother Branham. He revealed the secrets of the heart, showing the presence of the Son of man with his ministry. If the Son of man is here in Spirit form, what means is he using to reveal himself? Let us look more closely.

The Bride Coming to the Fullness of Christ

An important Scripture attached to this event is what the apostle Paul states: that the church comes to the point where she has reached "the measure of the stature of the fullness of Christ." Let's expand this and look at the entire prophecy given by the apostle Paul.

Ephesians 4:11-13 *"[11] And he gave some, apostles; and some, prophets; and some, evangelists; and some, pastors and teachers; [12] For the perfecting of the saints, for the work of the ministry, for the edifying of the body of Christ: [13] Till we all come in the unity of the faith, and of the knowledge of the Son of God, unto a perfect man, unto the measure of the stature of the fullness of Christ:"*

First, Paul is explaining that Christ gave apostles, prophets, evangelists, pastors and teachers for the perfecting of the saints. He then goes on to say that he is doing this

"until ..." The word "until" speaks of time: it means up to a certain point. The giving of these ministry gifts is to bring us up to the point that we come to the unity of the faith, the knowledge of the Son of God, unto a perfect or mature man, the stature of the fullness of Christ. This word "until" illustrates that this work will continue to mature up to the point that the bride is raptured. Once she has reached full maturity in this union with Christ, the rapture takes place. The church, or bride, will come to the place that she is expressing everything that Christ is.

Ephesians 5:25-32 *"25 Husbands, love your wives, even as Christ also loved the church, and gave himself for it; 26 That he might sanctify and cleanse it with the washing of water by the word, 27 That he might present it to himself a glorious church, not having spot, or wrinkle, or any such thing; but that it should be holy and without blemish. 28 So ought men to love their wives as their own bodies. He that loveth his wife loveth himself. 29 For no man ever yet hated his own flesh; but nourisheth and cherisheth it, even as the Lord the church: 30 For we are members of his body, of his flesh, and of his bones. 31 For this cause shall a man leave his father and mother, and shall be joined unto his wife, and they two shall be one flesh. 32 This is a great mystery: but I speak concerning Christ and the church."*

Christ promises that he will cleanse and perfect his bride with the Word. As the Word is revealed to us as individuals it cleanses and sanctifies us. Scripture denotes that he will present his church or bride to himself without spot or wrinkle. So, he will have a bride that is perfect, completely restored to the original faith and in possession of the true revealed Word. It is not a denominational, partial word, but the full Word as revealed in Scripture. Then we notice Paul is writing and informing us that the bride are members of his body, of his flesh and of his bones. Therefore, we conclude that the church is Christ in bride form. Is the body of Christ different from Christ? Absolutely not. She, the bride, is Him!

"And as He, being the Groom, the Bride has to come forth, 'cause It's part of Him. And It can only be the manifestation of the fulfilling of all the revelations any others has spoke of the Bride; It can only manifest. If it does something different from the Groom, it isn't the Bride. Because, She is flesh of His flesh, bone of His bone; Life of His Life, Power of His Power! She is Him!" [xviii]

This cannot come, but at the end time, when the book is opened and revealed. The bride is now washed, cleansed, and since he has come down now this bride is the fullness of Christ. In the sermon "Invisible Union" Brother Branham confirms this:

"What is it? Just exactly like the same grain that went in the ground, the same Jesus in the Bride form, same power, same Church, same thing, same Word." [xix]

When you look at this glorious church without spot or wrinkle you are seeing Christ manifested. She is not Jesus, but she is the visible manifestation of Jesus Christ to the world. Let's go further under the seventh seal and see the work the bride is to do.

Eat the Book

Revelation 10:8-11 *"⁸ And the voice which I heard from heaven spake unto me again, and said, 'Go and take the little book which is open in the hand of the angel which standeth upon the sea and upon the earth.' ⁹ And I went unto the angel, and said unto him, 'Give me the little book.' And he said unto me, 'Take it, and eat it up; and it shall make thy belly bitter, but it shall be in thy mouth sweet as honey.' ¹⁰ And I took the little book out of the angel's hand, and ate it up; and it was in my mouth sweet as honey: and as soon as I had eaten it, my belly was bitter. ¹¹ And he said unto me, 'Thou must prophesy again before many peoples, and nations, and tongues, and kings.'"*

As we have already established, this book is to be opened and revealed in the end time. It is the Mighty Angel that descends to bring this open book and communicates it through seven thunders unto the seventh church age messenger, Brother Branham. Then we see that John is offered the book and it is given to him to eat. This book begins a transforming process: it was delicious to eat, but was bitter in his belly. It brought conviction and transformation. Then, John is told to prophesy again among the Gentiles and the nations of the earth. This prophesy was not altogether given solely to the apostle John. Though John had his part of it, John was representing the recipients of this open book, which is the wise, who will understand at the end time, which, in fact, is the bride. Notice what Brother Branham writes:

"God raised up others and so it has gone on through the years until in this last day there is again another people in the land, who under their messenger will be the final voice to the final age." [xx]

The bride is given this open book to eat and make the vitamins and minerals of it become a part of her. This washes her and cleanses her so that she is without spot or wrinkle [ie-"many shall be purified and made white and tried"-Daniel 12:10] and then she is given a work to do: to bring the prophesy of this book to all nations. It must be a gentile bride bringing a message of the open book to a gentile people, looking for that last predestinated seed so that we can be caught up to heaven for the Marriage Supper of the Lamb.

Conclusion

1. The Mighty Angel descends with an open book and utters his voice (corresponding to 1 Thessalonians 4:16, the Lord himself shall descend from heaven with a shout, with the voice of the archangel and the trump of God)

2. The Seven Thunders utter their voices (this corresponds to the seven angels that met bro. Branham on Sunset Mountain in Arizona)

3. The Seventh messenger brings a message to finish the mystery of God as contained in the sealed book

We trust that this is a blessing to you, as you grow in the Word of God. This is such a monumental move of God in the end-time and we are so grateful to be a part of it. There is a vindicated word that's been revealed in this hour. Our souls are tied to it. How the love of God should be shed abroad in our hearts in this day, as we have witnessed, through the Message, Christ unveiling himself to us.

ADDENDUM
Significance of the Opening of the Seven Sealed Book

I would like to take a few moments of your time to discuss the significance of the opening of the Seven Seals in the book of Revelation chapter 5.

As believers of the end time Message, we rejoice that the seals have been opened and revealed to us by the grace of God. In 1963 the seals were opened by the Lord Jesus and then revealed to us by the prophet, William Marrion Branham, of Malachi 4:5-6.

This is a tremendous Biblical event which leads to John weeping when he discovers that no one is worthy to loose the seals and open the book. It sparks a Pentecostal revival in heaven of shouting and rejoicing that, indeed, one was found worthy. This should give us a moment to pause and consider the significance of this book and its contents.

In verse 3 we find exactly that, no man in heaven, earth or the grave was found worthy to claim or open the seven seals.

A review of the scriptures, may help us to fully grasp the reality of its contents.

Revelation 5:1-4 *"¹ And I saw in the right hand of him that sat on the throne a book written within and on the backside, sealed with seven seals. ² And I saw a strong angel proclaiming with a loud voice, Who is worthy to open the book, and to loose the seals thereof? ³ And no man in heaven, nor in earth, neither under the earth, was able to open the book, neither to look thereon. ⁴ And I wept much, because no man was found worthy to open and to read the book, neither to look thereon."*

We need to determine what this book is. As we do so, let's examine each aspect of these verses. The book is the in the right hand which signifies power or authority. John saw this book in the right hand of God himself, the original owner of all things. The KJV calls it a book, but it is a scroll, as were the ancient means of writing. The book was written within and on the backside. The normal procedure is that the book would just have writing inside of it. But this scroll has writing inside and out. This seems to signify to us that there is a great deal of information contained within the scroll. In verse 1 we see that the scrolls (book) was sealed with seven seals. As illustrated above, there are seven sheets of paper, each having been sealed.

In verse 2 there is a strong angel asking the question, "Who is worthy to open the book and to loose the seals?" This verse shows us that the book has a specific purpose and it cannot be opened by merely anyone. Since the book was in the hands of God we deem that the book itself is not even for God, himself, the eternal and invisible Spirit to open. The strong angel made the proclamation and so we assume that this book is not even for the angels. A man must be found worthy to open the book.

In verse 3 we find exactly that, no man in heaven, earth or the grave was found worthy to claim and open the book. The 24 elders were not found worthy; John was not worthy; and neither were any of the prophets of old. No one was worthy. As a result, in verse 4, John weeps much. The word "weep" means to sob or wail aloud. This was not on the order of alligator tears and loud lamentations. All humor aside, this book was so significant that it caused John to lose all hope that no one was found worthy. The next word is "much," in the sense that John "wept much," however, this word could also mean "many." That is, many around the throne wept because of no one being found worthy. What is the significance of this book? Let's keep reading in the scriptures.

Revelation 5:5-6 *"⁵ And one of the elders saith unto me, "Weep not: behold, the Lion of the tribe of Juda, the Root of David, hath prevailed to open the book, and to loose the seven seals thereof. ⁶ And I beheld, and, lo, in the midst of the throne and of the four beasts, and in the midst of the elders, stood a Lamb as it had been slain, having seven horns and seven eyes, which are the seven Spirits of God sent forth into all the earth."*

Amen! One of the elders informed John that he need not weep. There was a solution to the problem and the need, to open and reveal the contents of the book. The elder informs him that the lion of the tribe of Judah, the root of David has prevailed. The role that Jesus Christ plays as the lion signifies him as King of kings and Lord of lords in his position during the millennial reign. It purports that judgment is coming and that the kingdom is at hand. It says that the lion has prevailed, subdued or conquered, to open the book and loose the seals thereof. To have the right to claim and open the book, you had to conquer. Prior to this time, in the book of Revelation, John had not seen the Lamb at all. Then out of nowhere, standing in the middle of the scene of the throne, amidst the four beasts and the elders was a lamb that had been slain. John was told a lion had prevailed and when he looked there was a Lamb standing in the midst of the throne and beasts and elders as it had been slain. He had been hidden from the scene. He had been seated to make intercessions "for the ignorance of the people." This is the role of Jesus Christ as intercessor. This hearkens back to the work of the high priest on the Day of Atonement. He took the blood into the most holy place and sprinkled the mercy seat seven times. Each sin had a specific sacrifice attached to it, therefore, when the people knew of their sin they were to make an offering as quickly as possible. But for those sins done in ignorance, the high priest went in once a year and made an atonement for them.

Jesus Christ had fulfilled his time as an intercessor and now stands to claim his rightful possession, the seven-sealed scroll. It is understood that Christ is neither a literal lion or a literal lamb. These are prophetic symbols, metaphors. Jesus does not appear slain now, he is in his resurrected body, only with pierced hands and feet, to remind us of his work of redemption for us. Jesus does not have seven eyes and seven horns. These are also symbols. Christ has seven spirits that are sent forth into all the earth. These are seven messengers that are sent out with specific work to do.

The weeping of John leads us to understand the extreme significance of this book. The connection of this book to someone being worthy to open it, brings it more into the light. Let's continue in the chapter to get the full sense of the purpose of this seven-sealed book.

Revelation 5:7-10 *"⁷ And he came and took the book out of the right hand of him that sat upon the throne. ⁸ And when he had taken the book, the four beasts and four and twenty elders fell down before the Lamb, having every one of them harps, and golden vials full of odours, which are the prayers of saints. ⁹ And they sung a new song, saying, Thou art worthy to take the book, and to open the seals thereof: for thou wast slain, and hast redeemed us to God by thy blood out of every kindred, and tongue, and people, and nation; ¹⁰ And hast made us unto our God kings and priests: and we shall reign on the earth."*

The Lord Jesus Christ came forward to take the book out of the hand of God. The man, Christ Jesus, had been interceding for our sins before the throne of God and now he stands in the midst of the throne, beasts, and elders and then comes forward to claim the book as his own. This is a prophetic book and this is a prophetic scene that John witnesses. He was not seeing a contemporary event, but a prophetic one to take place at the end of the age. It must be so, as we look at the words of God to Daniel.

Daniel 12:4 *"But thou, O Daniel, shut up the words, and seal the book, even to the time of the end: many shall run to and fro, and knowledge shall be increased."*

Daniel 12:8-10 *"[8] And I heard, but I understood not: then said I, O my Lord, what shall be the end of these things? [9] And he said, 'Go thy way, Daniel: for the words are closed up and sealed till the time of the end. [10] Many shall be purified, and made white, and tried; but the wicked shall do wickedly: and none of the wicked shall understand; but the wise shall understand.'"*

In 1963 as Brother Branham prepared himself to receive the revelation of each of these seals the Lamb came forward and made his redemption claim. It is only at the time of the end that this book will be opened and its contents revealed. It remained a hidden mystery until the last, and seventh, church age. The angels and the elders fell down to worship the Lamb of God and their song of worship was: "you are worthy to take the book and open the seals because you were slain and have redeemed us to God by your blood." The word redeemed in the Greek is agorazo, and it means, "to purchase." Jesus paid the purchase price for us. But there is a second part to redemption and that is to claim your property. You first pay the price and then you claim your property. Redemption was not complete at Calvary. The price was paid, but the claim was not made. Notice what Paul writes to the Ephesians: ***Ephesians 4:30*** *"And* *grieve not the holy Spirit of God, whereby ye are sealed unto the day of redemption."* The day of redemption was a future time in the days of Paul. Look at what Peter writes: **1 Peter 1:5** *"Who are kept by the power of God through faith unto salvation ready to be revealed in the last time."*

Here we see salvation as something that will be revealed to the church in the end time. This is precisely connected with the words given Daniel. There will be an opening of the sealed book at the end time and it will cause that many shall be purified and made white and the wise will understand it.

This book, therefore, is the title deed of redemption, containing the names of the redeemed and the mysteries of redemption to be revealed in the last time. He died to purchase the right to this book and its contents. Without taking the book all was lost. The Lamb takes the book and breaks the seals one by one. He looses them and John then writes down a vision connected to each of them. In 1963, Brother Branham revealed the meaning of each of them. This could only happen when those seals were opened. As soon as the seventh seal is broke open, the whole book can be revealed

The significance of the seven-sealed book is that it is the title deed to redemption and it contains the names of all the redeemed and the mysteries of redemption that must be made known in the end-time in order to complete the work of redemption. When Jesus Christ claims, opens and reveals the book then he is no longer interceding for the ignorance of the people. The whole mystery is made known and revealed. Ignorance cannot be claimed anymore. There is always grace and mercy for God's elect, but now in the plan of redemption, there has been a transition. Salvation has been revealed in the last time. We no longer have a Lamb as though it had been slain, awaiting the time to make redemption claims. Revelation 10 shows us the whole picture.

We notice in Revelation 10, that in 1963, Christ comes down in Angelic form with an open book, seven thunders utter their voices and the seventh angel messenger reveals the mystery of God and then this book is given to John, representing the Bride, and she is to eat the book. The fact that it is an open book shows that once, it had been sealed. Now, Christ comes down to reveal that book and it comes from seven thunders down to the seventh angel messenger, William Branham. The book goes from the hands of the one that claimed it, Christ, and is given to his Bride to eat. *She is to become one with the book.* This is clearly a new phase of redemption. If we don't eat the open book then we aren't experiencing the full process of redemption that Christ paid for at Calvary. If we refuse to eat this book we are refusing the atonement made by Jesus Christ.

BIBLIOGRAPHY

i. E200- And I was at Tucson, Arizona, in the vision, for it made it so purpose that He didn't want me to fail to see where it was at. I was picking a sand burr off of me, from the desert. And I said, "Now, I know this is a vision, and I know that I'm at Tucson. And I know that them little birds there represent something." And they were watching eastward. And all of a sudden they taken a notion to fly, and away they went, eastward.

E201- And as soon as they left, a constellation of larger birds came. They looked like doves, sharp-pointed wings, kind of a gray color, little lighter color than what these first little messengers was. And they were coming eastward, swiftly.

E202- And no sooner than they got out of my sight, I turned again to look westward, and there it happened. There was a blast that actually shook the whole earth.

E203- Now, don't miss this. And you, on tape, be sure you get this right.

E204- First, a blast. And I thought it sounded like a sound barrier, ever what you call it when planes cross the sound, and the sound comes back to the earth. Just shook, like, roared, everything. Then, it could have been a—a—a great clap of thunder, and lightning, like; I didn't see the lightning. I just heard that great blast that went forth, that sounded like it was south, from me, towards Mexico.

E205- But, it shook the earth. And when it did, I was still looking westward. And way off into Eternity, I saw a constellation of something coming. It looked like that it might have been little dots. There could have been no less than five, and not more than seven. But, They were in the shape of a pyramid, like these messengers coming. And when it did, the Power of Almighty God lifted me up to meet Them. 206 And I can see It. It's never left me. Eight days has gone, and I can't forget it, yet. I never had anything to bother me like that has. My family will tell you. 207 I could see those Angels, those shaped-back wings, traveling faster than sound could travel. They come from Eternity, in a split, like a twinkling of an eye. Not enough to bat your eye, just a twinkle, They were there. I didn't have time to count. I didn't have time no more than just look. Mighty Ones, great, powerful Angels, snow white; wings set, and heads. And They were, "Whew-whew!" And when it did, I was caught up into this pyramid, a constellations.
62-1230E, Is This The Sign Of The End, Sir?, William Branham

ii. But, They were in the shape of a pyramid, like these messengers coming. And when it did, the Power of Almighty God lifted me up to meet Them.
62-1230E, Is This The Sign Of The End, Sir?, William Branham

iii. And just as I looked, right there was them Angels just

as plain as They could be, setting right there in that picture. See? I looked to see when it was, and it was time, same, about day or two before, or, day or two after I was up there. I looked where it was at. "Northeast of Flagstaff, or Prescott, which is below Flagstaff." Well, that's just where we was at, see, just exactly. "Twenty-six miles high." Why, vapor can't go over—over four, four miles high, or five, moisture, any kind of fog or anything, you see. Planes fly at nineteen thousand. That's to get up above all the clouds, you see. And nineteen thousand is about four miles high. This is twenty-six miles high, and thirty miles across it, and in the shape of the pyramid, if you've looked at the picture.

63-0601, Come, Follow Me, William Branham

iv. And so I must not take what anyone says; I must—it must be inspired. And I believe that the Seven Angels who's holds these seven thunders will grant it.

63-0317M, God Hiding Himself In Simplicity, Then Revealing Himself In The Same, William Branham

I seen the rocks tumbling off the side of the hill, rolling down. And I looked up, there was that white Circle above me there, circling around. Here come seven Angels, come moving down out of the air, picked me up, and said, "Go back to your home, to the East, right away, and bring those Seven Seals. For, there is seven mysteries, for the complete Word is revealed now in these seven mysteries."

63-0802, Perseverant, William Branham

v. 63-0317E, The Breach Between The Seven Church Ages And The Seven Seals, William Branham

vi. 63-0323, The Sixth Seal, William Branham

vii. Now, God had a purpose and a hidden mystery. And that's what I want to speak on to the Church this morning, the hidden mystery of God that He had in His mind before the world ever began, and how that it's unfolded itself right down to this present hour that we're living. See? Then you will understand clearly then, you see, on, I believe, what is being done. 106 God's great mystery of how, it's a secret. He kept it a secret. Nobody knowed nothing about it. Even the Angels didn't understand it. See, He didn't reveal it. That's the reason, under our seventh mystery, when the seventh seal was opened, there was silence. Jesus, when He was on earth, they wanted to know when He would come. He said, "It's not... Even the Son Himself don't know when it's going to happen." See, God has this all to Himself. It's a secret. And that's the reason there was silence in Heaven for a space of a half hour, and seven thunders utter their voices, and John was even forbidden to write it, see, the Coming of the Lord. That's one thing He hasn't revealed yet, of how He will come, and when He will come. It's a good thing that He doesn't. No. He has showed or revealed it in every type that's in the Bible. Therefore, the entire Bible is the revelation of God's mystery in Christ. Hum! The entire Bible is an expression of one goal that God had, one purpose He wanted to achieve in the entire Bible. And all the acts of the—of the believers in the Bible has been in type, and expressing what God's great goal is, and now in this last day He has revealed it and shows it. And God's help, well, you'll see it right here this morning, what the Lord has had in His mind all along, and has expressed it. 63-0728, Christ Is The Mystery Of God Revealed, William Branham

viii. 65-1204, The Rapture, William Branham

ix. Luke 16:16

x. An Exposition of the Seven Church Ages, Laodicean Church Age, Chapter 9, William Branham

xi. 63-0318, The First Seal, William Branham

xii. 62-1230M, Absolute, William Branham

xiii. 63-0317E, The Breach, William Branham

xiv. 64-0719M, Feast of the Trumpets, William Branham

xv. 63-0318, The First Seal, William Branham

xvi. 64-0614M, Unveiling of God, William Branham

xvii. 64-0830E, Questions & Answers, William Branham

xviii. 65-0418M, It Is The Rising Of The Sun, William Branham

xix. 65-1125, The Invisible Union Of The Bride Of Christ, William Branham

xx. An Exposition Of The Seven Church Ages, Chapter Nine, The Laodicean Church Age, William Branham

Made in the USA
Columbia, SC
09 April 2024